SKIES ABOVE THE CARIBBEAN

by Jannine Mahone

I dedicate this book to every curious 8-year-old (and every kid at heart) who's ever looked up at a plane in the sky and wondered where it was going ...

This book is for you.

May it remind you that big dreams can start with small wishes, and that one day, the skies you look up to might just carry you toward your own amazing adventure.

Jamaica

Life in the countryside of Jamaica was full of fun and adventure.

My cousins and I climbed trees to pick ripe fruits, built kites and flew them high in the wind, and spent hours playing with marbles, trucks, and dolls. But my favorite thing of all was looking up at the sky every time a plane flew overhead. I'd wonder, "Where is that plane going?" I dreamed about faraway places I had only read about in books. One day, I promised myself: When I grow up, I'm going to travel the world.

But even though I dreamed of going far, living in Jamaica was amazing too. Did you know the island is over 4,000 square miles and has 14 parishes? A parish is almost like a state in the USA.

Jamaica has over 50 stunning beaches to explore, some with white sand, others with gleaming black sand! Kids in town loved riding their bikes, but in the countryside with hills, we built go-carts and raced them down the road.

My name is Jannine, and I'm going to take you on my adventures around the world!

United States

My first trip outside of Jamaica was to Texas, in the United States.

I thought I'd see cowboys, horses, and cows everywhere, like in the movies! Instead, I saw huge highways, millions of cars, and grocery stores that were so big, I worried I would get lost. In Jamaica, we had local markets with lots of crafts and fresh food. The supermarkets were way smaller!

One of my favorite memories was riding a boat down the Riverwalk in San Antonio. I listened to mariachi music and visited the Alamo, an old fort with a big story behind it.

Did you know Texas is the second largest state in the U.S.? The smallest state, Rhode Island, can fit into Texas over 200 times! Texas also has beautiful beaches. I went fishing off the pier in Galveston with my family. We didn't catch many fish, but we had lots of fun trying!

United Kingdom | England

I've always loved the royal family, so visiting Buckingham Palace felt like a dream.

One summer I visited my cousins in London, and we did all kinds of cool stuff. We rode on red double-decker buses and the London subway, which they call "the Tube." We walked past Big Ben (a very tall clock tower!), watched the ducks in Kew Gardens, and even visited the British Museum to see ancient treasures.

One day we had "high tea," which is when you sit at a fancy table and drink tea from real teacups and eat tiny sandwiches and sweet cakes. I felt very fancy!

The weather was a little chilly and cloudy most days, so I always needed my jacket - even in the summer.

Did you know that the United Kingdom isn't just one country? It's made up of England, Scotland, Wales, and Northern Ireland. London is in England, but when people say "UK," they mean all four countries together. London is full of people from all over the world. I heard so many languages, and I even saw food from places like India, Africa, and China.

United Kingdom | Scotland

Scotland was full of history and adventure.

We visited Edinburgh castle where Mary, Queen of Scots, once lived! It felt like stepping into a storybook because the stone walls were so big and old. Scotland has over 2,000 castles, and many of them are open for people to visit. Some even sit on cliffs or beside lakes!

The countryside was rugged and green, and the people were so friendly. Their Scottish accents made everything sound cooler. I even heard someone playing bagpipes in the street. The music was loud and uplifting! Some men still wear kilts, which are like colorful skirts made of tartan (a special checked fabric). Every Scottish family has its own tartan pattern!

Scottish food is unique! I heard about haggis (it's made with sheep organs), but I didn't try it. I stuck to regular foods like soup and bread, and that was just fine with me.

It's easy to travel around the United Kingdom. We took trains between cities and they were fast and comfortable. Did you know the countries in the United Kingdom - England, Scotland, Wales, and Northern Ireland - are all close together? You don't even need a plane to go from London to Scotland!

The Netherlands

My friends and I wandered the streets of Amsterdam and loved the culture.

We walked on cobblestone streets and crossed little bridges over the canals. The water was everywhere. It's seems like the city floats! People riding bikes is common here so they were everywhere. I had to look both ways to stay safe. The buildings were tall and skinny, and some of them looked like gingerbread houses.

Amsterdam is in a country called the Netherlands, which is famous for windmills, wooden shoes called clogs, and fields full of colorful tulips. I saw tulips in gardens, in flower shops, and even painted on souvenirs. I even found a pair of giant wooden clogs big enough to stand in!

One thing I loved was hearing so many languages. Did you know Europe has over 200 languages? In Amsterdam alone, people spoke Dutch, English, German, French, and sometimes even Spanish, all on the same street! It felt like the entire world was in one city. In Jamaica, English is the language of business, but many Jamaicans also speak Jamaican Creole.

France

Paris looked like a museum - shiny, golden, and full of art.

Even some statues on the street had gold on them, which made everything feel rich and special. We walked along the Champs-Elysees, one of the most famous streets in the world, and took so many pictures! I even tried duck for the first time (it tasted better than I thought!), and I ate so many buttery, delicious croissants I lost count.

We got to see the Eiffel Tower up close and it is much taller and magnificent than you can imagine! At night it sparkled with lights. We also took a riverboat ride down the Seine, the famous river that flows through the middle of Paris. The buildings on both sides looked like paintings.

Did you know there's a tunnel called the Chunnel that goes under the ocean and connects England to France? These cities are so close you can take a train through the Chunnel to travel between them.

France is also famous for its artists like Monet and Degas, and for its fashion. People there dress nice even just to go outside! I felt like I was walking through a magazine.

Belgium

Belgium was like stepping into a flower-filled postcard.

We visited Brussels to see the Flower Carpet and learned that it took almost a million flowers to make. The streets were spotless, and I remember feeling safe walking around.

We ate the most delicious waffles, covered in whipped cream and fruit. I also bought Belgian chocolate to take home. It melted in my mouth like magic. Everywhere we went, it smelled like something sweet was baking. It reminded me of bakeries in my hometown in Jamaica, where you could smell bread and buns baking from far away!

Brussels had little canals and stone bridges that made it feel like a storybook town. I loved just strolling around and looking at everything. Belgium may be small, but it's full of beautiful surprises!

FESTIVAL OF FLOWERS

Germany

What I remember most about Munich, Germany, was the food, especially the sausages!

We had grilled sausages with spicy mustard, and they were delicious. Everywhere we walked, we found beautiful town squares with historic buildings and cobblestone streets. You could almost feel the history as you walked through the squares or "platz."

Germany includes different regions, each with its own traditions. One famous area is the Black Forest, where the yummy Black Forest cake comes from. It's made with chocolate, cherries, and whipped cream. I didn't get to eat a slice this time, but it looked amazing in the bakery windows!

One of the coolest things in Germany is the Autobahn, a special highway where some parts have no speed limit! German cars like BMW, Audi, and Mercedes zoom past super fast. It amazed me how quiet and smooth they seemed, even when traveling that fast.

Germany was full of old charm and modern excitement. I loved every bit.

Italy

Milan is the heart of fashion and even the graffiti looked cool!

People looked stylish and the city had a buzzing energy. We ate the best food in Milan. Not just pizza, but pasta, sandwiches, and fresh Italian treats called gelato. I tried a different flavor every day!

One of the most historic places our guide showed us was the Duomo di Milano, a giant church with tiny carvings and statues on the outside. The architecture was so detailed it made me wonder how they built it.

We also saw famous sculptures and paintings in the museums. Italy is known for its amazing art, and it felt like every corner of Milan was a gallery. Our guide took us to the walled city of Bergamo and beautiful Lake Como, where the water sparkled like glass.

Milan is close to Venice, where you can ride in gondolas which are long boats that float through canals instead of streets. We didn't go there this time, but now I want to!

The people in Milan were friendly and fun, and I felt like I could've stayed there forever.

Liechtenstein

Liechtenstein was the hardest country name for me to spell and to say!

It's pronounced "Lick-ten-stein," and it's one of the tiniest countries in the entire world. We stopped there only for a quick visit to get souvenirs, but I remember how super clean and quiet everything was. The buildings looked neat and perfect, like a postcard.

Even though it's small, Liechtenstein has its own royal family. The prince lives in Vaduz Castle, which sits on top of a hill. You can't go inside, but it looks amazing from the outside! I took lots of pictures and imagined what it would be like to live in an actual castle.

Liechtenstein lies between Switzerland and Austria, and people speak German there. I marveled at the serenity. We didn't stay long, but I'll always have special memories of it.

Switzerland

Switzerland felt like a travel dream come true like the kind you read about in books.

We visited Zurich, then took a motorcoach through the Alps, where the snowy mountains looked like giant scoops of ice cream. One of my favorite stops was Heidi House. Yes, the Heidi from the book written by Johanna Spyri! I loved reading that book! We saw goats, drank fresh milk, and everything felt simple and sweet. The air was fresh, with flowers and trees everywhere.

Nature was so vivid all around us with green hills, bright meadows, and peaceful farms with wooden houses. We even got to try real Swiss chocolate!

Switzerland is the home of Albert Einstein, one of the most famous scientists ever! He lived in Switzerland for a while and even became a citizen. That made me feel like smart people must love it there. Everything in Switzerland felt calm, organized, and beautiful. It's a place I would love to visit again!

HEIDI
HOUSE

Austria

Austria was like stepping into a music box, sweet and delightful.

We stayed in Vienna, which is famous for its music. The city was filled with art and beauty. It was surprisingly serene and not crowded, unlike other places I've been. Beautiful old buildings lined the streets, and the sound of music was everywhere, even played live in parks and plazas!

Vienna is home to famous composers like Mozart, Beethoven, and Strauss. We visited Mozart's birthplace in Salzburg, which felt like stepping back in time. I imagined him as a boy playing the piano for kings and queens!

Salzburg is where The Sound of Music was filmed. I sat in the real gazebo from the movie! The hills and mountains around the city were green and lush, just like in the film.

In Vienna, I tried Sachertorte, the most famous dessert in Austria! It's a rich chocolate cake with apricot jam inside, and whipped cream on the side. I felt fancy when I ordered it!

Austria felt calm and simple, but full of creativity. It made me want to learn to play an instrument - or maybe even sing out loud in the mountains!

Ireland

Ireland was my favorite place to visit. It felt like several storybooks wrapped into one.

We rode on a ferry from Holyhead in Wales to Dublin. The water was choppy! I held on tight and felt so relieved when we reached land!

Ireland is known for its soft hills, stone walls, and bright yellow wildflowers called gorse. We stayed at a cozy bed-and-breakfast in Killarney where the people were kind and welcoming. They were cheerful and made me feel at home.

We explored the Ring of Kerry where we saw sheep-covered hills, cliffs overlooking the ocean, and winding roads that looked like they'd go on forever. In Cobh, we saw the Titanic's last stop before sailing to America and row houses painted in bright colors that looked like a postcard.

Ireland has over 30,000 castles and ruins, and each one looked mysterious, like it held secrets from the past. We heard the beautiful voices of Irish tenors singing traditional songs. Their voices were powerful and gave me goosebumps. Ireland felt like a song, a painting, and a dream rolled into one!

Wales

We passed through Wales on our way to catch the ferry to Ireland, and even though we didn't stay long, I still remember it.

The English countryside we drove through was green and brown, with rolling hills, tiny villages, and lots of sheep! When we crossed into Wales, the signs changed and some words were so long I couldn't even try to pronounce them. Welsh is a proper language, and it sounds entirely different!

The people had a gentle, musical accent, and even though we were just passing through, I loved hearing them speak. I read about one town with 58 letters in its name! Now that would be hard to fit on a postcard!

The quick stop inspired me to go back and explore more someday.

Llanfairpwllgwyngyllgo
gerychwyrndrobwllllant
ysiliogogogoch

Australia

Australia felt like a series of giant adventures from the moment we landed in Sydney!

The Sydney Opera House looked like a giant ship with white sails rising out of the water. We didn't go inside, but we sailed right past it on a yacht in Sydney Harbour and it looked more majestic up close.

One of my favorite places was the zoo, where we saw giraffes, elephants, kangaroos, and koalas! Koalas are amazing animals. They sleep for almost 20 hours a day and move slowly, as though they have all the time in the world.

We spent the day at Manly Beach, where the sand was golden and the water was clear and blue. We even played a game of cricket on the sand. It's a popular sport in Australia, kind of like baseball but with different rules. My dad loved listening to cricket games on the radio in Jamaica, where most folks would cheer for the West Indies team.

Australia also has a rich history. I loved hearing the stories of the Aboriginal people, indigenous people who lived there first. Their art, music, and traditions are beautiful and full of meaning.

Mexico

Mexico was full of colors, music, and amazing food. The kind that makes your eyes light up and your heart feel happy.

I visited Mexico City, Cancun, and Cozumel, and each place had something special. In Mexico City, I stayed at a hotel where my favorite band was staying too! I couldn't believe it when I saw the lead singer in the lobby! I tried to stay calm, but inside I was thrilled.

The food in Mexico was delicious. I got to try different dishes with mole sauce, a thick sauce made sometimes with chocolate, spices, and chilies. Each type tasted a little different, and I learned mole is a big part of traditional Mexican cuisine.

In Cozumel, I went snorkeling in the ocean and saw colorful fish swimming through coral reefs. The water was clear and the palm trees along the beach looked like they were waving in the breeze. In the local market, women sold bright woven blankets in every color you can imagine. I also had fun trying on silver jewelry. The bracelets and rings sparkled in the sunlight.

Mexico was warm, exciting, and full of beautiful things to see and taste.

WORD SEARCH

A	I	R	P	O	R	T	R	S	W
I	T	F	F	D	R	R	A	U	C
R	R	I	L	A	D	A	S	I	A
P	E	D	O	N	A	V	I	T	K
L	E	W	W	C	U	E	L	C	E
A	S	D	E	I	S	L	O	A	L
N	S	I	R	N	T	O	I	S	T
E	A	I	S	G	A	R	D	E	N
C	O	U	N	T	R	Y	G	N	T
E	W	B	A	L	L	O	O	N	R

AIRPORT	**FLOWERS**	**COUNTRY**	**DANCING**
AIRPLANE	**BALLOON**	**TRAVEL**	**TREES**
GARDEN	**CAKE**	**SUITCASE**	**STAR**

DOT-TO-DOT

Begin at number 1 and connect the dots until the picture is complete.

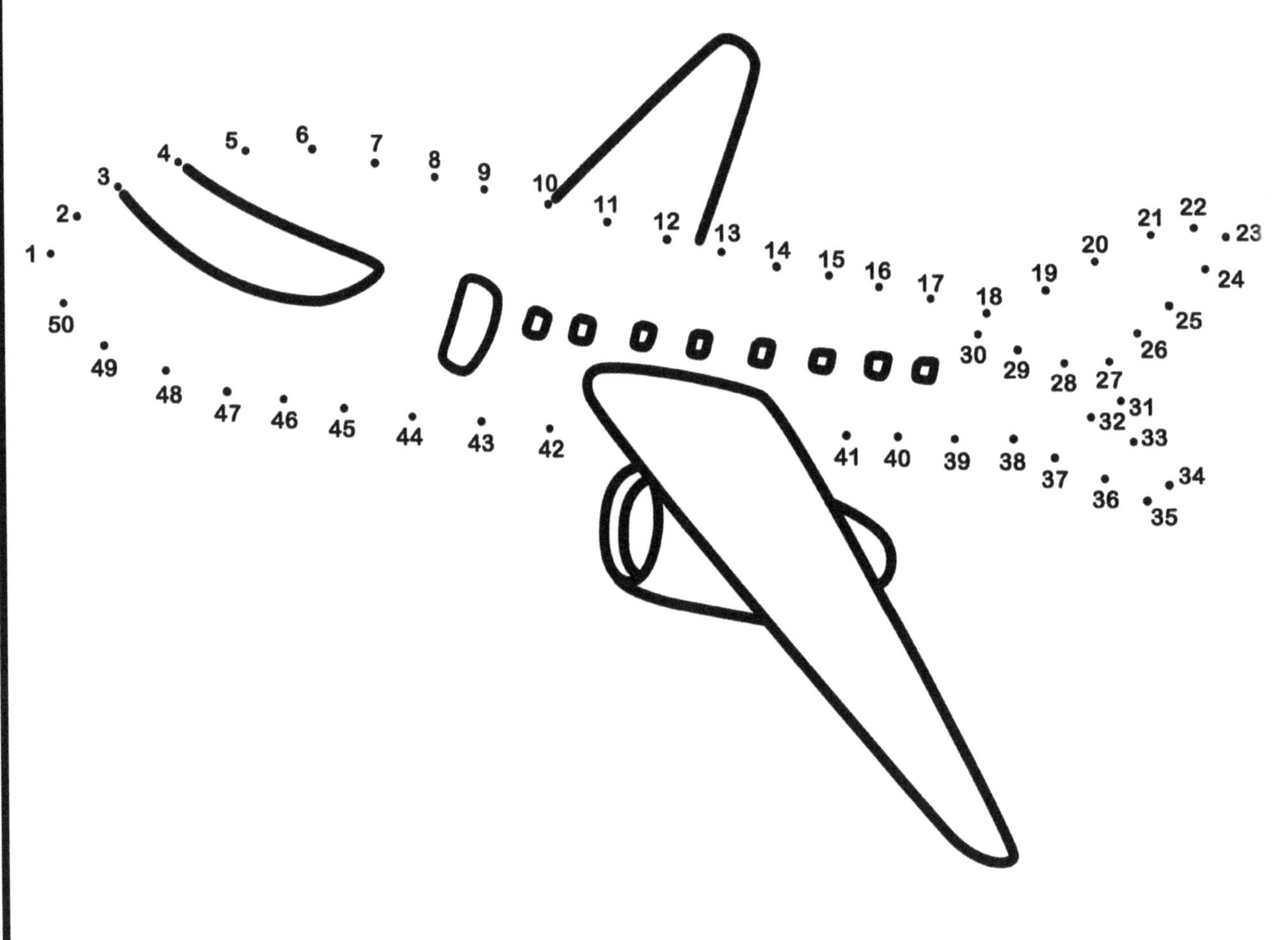

About the Author | Jannine Mahone

Jannine is an explorer, storyteller, and firsttime author who believes the world is one big colorful classroom. From climbing castles in Ireland to swimming with sting-rays in the Cayman Islands, she's turned her real-life adventures into this exciting trav-el-inspired coloring book just for you.

Born with a curious mind and a pass-port always ready to go, Jannine created *Skies Above the Caribbean* to help kids discover the magic of different places through stories, pictures, and imagination. She's especially proud of her Jamaican roots and the island's rich culture, music, and natural beauty, which inspired many of the pages in this book.

When she's not flying to her next destination, Jannine lives in Texas, where she works in technology, runs businesses, builds big dreams, and plans her next adventure.

Skies Above the Caribbean is her very first book-made with love for little travelers and future world-changers everywhere.

Published by
**WILT & WADE
PUBLISHING**
wiltandwade.com

ISBN: 979-8-9896694-5-5

Printed in the United States of America